PRENTICE HALL'S GUIDE

to

UNDERSTANDING PLAGIARISM

Thomas Jewell

D0139767

PEARSON
Prentice
Hall

Upper Saddle River, New Jersey 07458

© 2004 by PEARSON EDUCATION, INC.
Upper Saddle River, New Jersey 07458

10 9 8 7 6 5 4 3

ISBN 0-13-144358-5

Printed in the United States of America

Table of Contents

Preface (What is this plagiarism tutorial all about, anyway?)

Chances are pretty good that your college catalog has a section on academic honesty that includes a warning about what can happen to a student who is caught plagiarizing. Depending on your school's policy, and your instructor, the penalties for plagiarism run from a failing grade on a plagiarized paper to failing a course to being expelled from school. Most colleges and most professors frown on plagiarism.

It may not even matter that your plagiarism is unintentional. If you use a source of information that you don't properly identify or cite, you are guilty of plagiarism whether you meant to omit it or not. How severely you can be punished, even for unintentional plagiarism, will depend largely on your instructor and the policies of your academic institution.

The main purposes of this tutorial are
1. to help you understand what plagiarism is, and
2. to help teach you how to avoid committing plagiarism.

Along the way, we'll also show you how to
1. properly attribute sources you use in your papers
2. properly quote material
3. accurately summarize material
4. carefully paraphrase material, and
5. how to cite and attribute information retrieved from electronic or other unconventional sources.

Finally, we'll give you a list of Internet sites where you can learn more about plagiarism and how to avoid it, as well as some sites to help you use proper bibliographic and other reference citations.

What is plagiarism?

Simply put, **plagiarism is using someone else's words and ideas in a paper and acting as though they are your own**. This definition includes copying someone else's ideas, graphs, pictures, or anything that you borrow without giving credit to the originator of the words and ideas. It definitely includes anything you download from an Internet site or copy out of a book, a newspaper, or a magazine. It also includes stealing the ideas of another person without giving them proper credit.

Some obvious examples of plagiarism include
- copying someone else's paper.
- taking short or long quotations from a source without identifying the source.
- turning in a paper you bought over the Internet.

Some less-obvious examples include
- changing a few words around from a book or article and pretending those words are your own.
- rearranging the order of ideas in a list and making the reader think you produced the list.
- borrowing ideas from a source and not giving proper credit to the source.
- turning in a paper from another class. Whether this is plagiarism or not depends on your instructor—ask first!
- using information from an interview or an online chat or email, etc., without properly citing the source of the information.
- using words that were quoted in one source and acting and citing the original source as though you read it yourself.

The ironic thing about committing plagiarism is that most professors prefer that you use quoted material and properly cite it. They want you to come up with your own ideas in a paper, but will usually give you a good deal of credit for the quality and quantity of outside sources you use as well. Learning how to give credit where credit is due is what this tutorial is all about, so it's time to get started.

Questions for "What is Plagiarism?"

1.　true or false?　As long as you change a few words around in a paragraph you read from one of your sources, you're not committing plagiarism.

　　　　true　Wrong! It is appropriate to paraphrase someone else's work, but simply changing a few words around is still plagiarism.

　　　　false　Right! It is appropriate to paraphrase someone else's work, but simply changing a few words around is still plagiarism.

2.　true or false?　If you find a list in one of your sources, it's OK to rearrange the list and claim it as your own as long as you at least leave one or two things off of the original list.

　　　　true　Wrong! To avoid plagiarism, if you borrow any part of a list from one of your sources, it should be properly attributed and cited.

　　　　false　Right! To avoid plagiarism, if you borrow any part of a list from one of your sources, it should be properly attributed and cited.

3.　true or false?　It's OK to copy an image from a book or an Internet site without identifying the original source.

　　　　true　Wrong! Any graph, picture, or other image taken from any source should be given proper credit.

　　　　false　Right! Any graph, picture, or other image taken from any source should be given proper credit.

4.　true or false?　As long as it otherwise meets the assignment and my professor doesn't tell me otherwise, it's OK to turn in a paper to one class that I originally did for another class.

　　　　true　Maybe. Whether or not turning in a paper that was used for another class is plagiarism depends on your instructor. You should always ask first to avoid trouble.

　　　　false　Maybe. Whether or not turning in a paper that was used for another class is plagiarism depends on your instructor. You should always ask first to avoid trouble.

5. true or false? I don't have to quote information I gathered by talking to a friend or someone I chatted with on the Internet.

   true   Wrong! Any time you use material gathered from another person or source, it needs to be properly identified and cited.

   false   Right! Any time you use material gathered from another person or source, it needs to be properly identified and cited.

Basic Rules for Avoiding Plagiarism

The Golden Rule for Avoiding Plagiarism—Give Credit Where Credit is Due

Basically, there is only one way to avoid plagiarism—**give credit to a source whenever you use information that is not your own unless it is common knowledge**. If you come up with an idea all on your own, you don't have to give credit to anyone, except yourself. Also, if you are writing about something that is common knowledge, you don't have to give a citation for your source.

Common Knowledge

Common knowledge is whatever information you and your reader is likely to know without referring to some other source. For example, there are 435 U.S. Congress Members and 100 U.S. Senators. That's probably common knowledge. How many of the Congress Members and Senators are Democrats, Republicans, or from other political parties, may or may not be common knowledge, depending on you and your reader(s). The more likely both you and your reader(s) are to know that information, and especially the more controversial a fact or idea is, the more likely it is to be common knowledge. How many votes any particular member of the House or the Senate got in the last election is probably not common knowledge. If the number of votes a candidate received in part of your paper, you should probably cite the source.

The best rule of thumb to determine whether or not to give credit to a source for information that might be common knowledge is, "When in doubt, give the source." It is always better to err on the safe side.

Cite Your Sources

When should you cite a source? **You should give credit to a source whenever you use someone else's work or idea that is not common knowledge.** This includes any time you use or refer to information that comes from

- interviews.
- Internet sites.
- chat room conversations.
- radio or television programs.
- personal letters.
- speeches.
- books.
- magazines.
- newspapers.
- tape, video, or CD recordings.
- electronic databases.
- basically any source.

Don't forget to give credit any time you use any of the following that come from another source:

- quotations
- statistics
- graphs
- pictures
- ideas or hypotheses
- stories
- lists

As stated above, the bottom line is that you have to provide a source citation for every use of another person's words or ideas unless the information is common knowledge.

Questions for "Basic Rules for Understanding and Avoiding Plagiarism":

1.   true or false   That George Bush is the President of the United States is common knowledge that wouldn't have to be cited in a paper.

        true   Right! Everyone should know this, so you don't have to reference it.

        false   Wrong. Everyone should know this, so you don't have to reference it

2.   true or false   The number of votes President Bush won in Florida during the 2000 election is so important that everyone should know it, so it would be common knowledge that wouldn't have to be cited in a paper.

        true   Wrong! This is specialized knowledge, and even if a lot of people know about it, the fact that many don't, coupled with how controversial the actual count was, would make it important to your reader to have the source of your information.

        false   Right! This is specialized knowledge, and even if a lot of people know about it, the fact that many don't, coupled with how controversial the actual count was, would make it important to your reader to have the source of your information.

3.   true or false   I didn't remember that Abraham Lincoln was the 16th President of the United States and that his Vice President was Ulysses S. Grant, so that information must not be common knowledge, which means I have to give a citation for it in my paper.

        true   Wrong! Information that is likely to be known by most people, even if they don't remember the specifics, probably doesn't require a citation unless it is controversial.

        false   Right! Information that is likely to be known by most people, even if they don't remember the specifics, probably doesn't require a citation unless it is controversial.

4.   true or false   When you're not sure about whether information in your paper is common knowledge or not, it's usually better not to cite a source, so your reader won't think you're trying to pad your paper with extra citations.

        true   Wrong! It's always better to err on the side of citing information that you're not certain is common knowledge.

        false   Right! It's always better to err on the side of citing information that you're not certain is common knowledge.

5. true or false You don't need to provide a citation for information you obtained in a conversation with a friend.

    true Wrong! Any information that is not your own or from common knowledge, must be cited, regardless of the source.

    false Right! Any information that is not your own or from common knowledge, must be cited, regardless of the source.

6. true or false You should provide a citation for a conversation you had in a chat room on the Internet.

    true Right! Any information that is not your own or from common knowledge, must be cited, regardless of the source.

    false Wrong! Any information that is not your own or from common knowledge, must be cited, regardless of the source.

7. true or false You don't need to provide a citation for a letter from a friend that you refer to in your paper, as long as you don't quote it.

    true Wrong! Any information that is not your own or from common knowledge, must be cited, regardless of the source.

    false Right! Any information that is not your own or from common knowledge, must be cited, regardless of the source.

8. true or false I heard a speaker in my history class talk about World War II. One of her ideas about the causes of the war was really interesting to me, but since I'm putting the idea in my own words, I don't need to provide a citation for the speaker.

    true Wrong! Any information that is not your own or from common knowledge, must be cited, regardless of the source, and regardless of whether or not the information is directly quoted.

    false Right! Any information that is not your own or from common knowledge, must be cited, regardless of the source, and regardless of whether or not the information is directly quoted.

9.   true or false   One of the guests on *Oprah* made a comment that I want to use in my paper about child abuse. Since I'm going to rephrase the comment anyway, I don't have to give a source citation.

        true   Wrong! Any information that is not your own or from common knowledge, must be cited, regardless of the source, and regardless of whether or not the information is directly quoted.

        false   Right! Any information that is not your own or from common knowledge, must be cited, regardless of the source, and regardless of whether or not the information is directly quoted.

10.   true or false   I came up with an idea for my paper on my own last week and wrote it down so I wouldn't forget it. Now, since it's in writing, I have to provide a source citation for the idea.

        true   Wrong! Since you came up with idea on your own, you don't have to give a source citation. Just be sure it wasn't an idea you read somewhere but forgot where it came from.

        false   Right! Since you came up with idea on your own, you don't have to give a source citation. Just be sure it wasn't an idea you read somewhere but forgot where it came from.

Attributing—Giving Credit Where Credit is Due

Attributing is the process of identifying the sources of your information within the paper that you're writing.

Attributing is a two-step process:
Step 1: Note each source as you use it in the body of your paper.
Step 2: Provide a complete source citation for every source you use.

Begin your understanding of proper attributing by reading the following excerpt from an article about a U.S. Supreme Court case, written by staff writer Warren Richey, found in the June 25, 2002 issue of the *Christian Science Monitor:*

> State judges may no longer make the key determination between life and death in capital-punishment cases without violating constitutional safeguards.
>
> In the second major capital-punishment ruling in less than a week, the US Supreme Court has struck down the sentencing procedures used in Arizona death-penalty cases, saying it violates the Sixth Amendment guarantee of a trial by jury.
>
> The court, in a 7-to-2 decision, drew a parallel between the sentencing system of Arizona (and by extension eight states with similar systems), and the sentence-enhancement system that the high court struck down two years ago in a landmark case called Apprendi v. New Jersey.
>
> The bottom line: A much anticipated revolution in criminal sentencing just became a lot more revolutionary.

STEP ONE: Identify Your Sources in the Body of Your Paper.

Sure, your professor may require you to include a bibliography or list of references at the end of your paper, or footnotes at the bottom of every page, or even both, but attributing properly requires you to identify your sources in the body of the paper as well.

The particular style manual that you're using will dictate what *must* appear as notice that an outside source is being used. The underlying principle is that the reader should be able to connect your source identification with a complete citation found at the appropriate place at the bottom of each page or at the end of your paper.

Style Manual	How You Note Sources in the Body of the Paper
MLA	• **For conventional sources** (with page numbers and authors), enclose the author's last name and the page number in parentheses. • **For electronic or other unconventional sources** (which often do not have page numbers or authors), name or describe the source within the text of the paper in a way that makes it easy for the reader to identify the source in your footnotes or at the end of your paper.
APA	Typically, you will name the author and place the date of publication in parentheses for example, Smith (1981) writes…. or both in parentheses One author (Smith 1981) writes…. . • You can add a page number for indirect references to an author's work and *must* include the page number for direct quotations. (Smith 1981, p. 47)
CMS	Put a raised number immediately after any quotation or other use of an outside source. Smith wrote that, "Nobody likes to be made or thought of as a fool."[1] or Smith wrote about what it is feels like to be thought of as a fool. [1] • If you're using "Endnotes", number each source consecutively throughout the body of the paper, starting with the number "1". • If you're using "Footnotes", number each source consecutively throughout each page, beginning with a new "1" at the bottom of each page which contains references.

CBE	Put a raised number or a number in parentheses, immediately after any quotation or other use of an outside source, numbered sequentially throughout the body of the paper. Smith wrote that, "Nobody likes to be made or thought of as a fool."[1] or Smith wrote about what it is feels like to be thought of as a fool.[1] • If you use more than one source to support an idea, use dashes for sources in sequence and commas for sources out of sequence. Several poets have argued that no one like to be thought of as a fool.[1-3] or Several poets have argued that no one likes to be thought of as a fool.[1-2, 5] • If you repeat a source later in the paper, use the original number.

Identify a source at the place in your paper where you use the source. Assume that you're writing a paper about the current state of the law regarding capital punishment in the United States. Further, assume that you want make your paper as up to date as possible by using information about the most recent Supreme Court case written about in this *Christian Science Monitor* article. At any point where you refer to the article, whether by quoting it, summarizing all or part of it, or paraphrasing parts of it, or just borrowing ideas from it, you must give credit to the source. The point is that you tell your reader where information you're giving them came from and that you make it easy for them to connect the source and the information by putting them close to one another in the text of your paper.

Incorrect Identification—the source is not identified in the body of the paper.

> One reporter recently wrote that, "The court . . . drew a parallel between the sentencing system of Arizona . . . and the sentence-enhancement system that the high court struck down two years ago in . . . Apprendi v. New Jersey."

Correct Identification—the source is identified in the body of the paper.

> Richey (2002) recently wrote that, "The court . . . drew a parallel between the sentencing system of Arizona . . . and the sentence-enhancement system that the high court struck down two years ago in . . . Apprendi v. New Jersey."

You will have to decide how much information to provide about a source in the body of your paper. Too much information about the source tends to clutter the point you're trying to make and to disrupt the flow of your prose. Too little information about the source may make your reader unsure of the quality of your research or fail to take advantage of the credibility that some sources will lend to the ideas you present in your paper.

Use Signal Phrases to Alert Your Reader to Your Use of Outside Sources.

One way to let your reader know that you're about to use an outside source is to use common phrases that readers expect to see before a quotation or other reference to the outside source. One author (Rasmussen 2003, p. 7) refers to these as signal phrases in the chart below and recommends that you carefully and accurately identify the intention of the source in your attribution.

Verbs Used in Signal Phrases

The verb you choose for a signal phrase should accurately reflect the intention of the source.

acknowledges	concedes	illustrates	reports
admits	concludes	implies	reveals
agrees	declares	insists	says
argues	denies	maintains	shows
believes	endorses	observes	suggests
claims	finds	points out	thinks
comments	grants	refutes	writes

Rasmussen, K. (2003). A writer's guide to research and documentation (5th ed.). Upper Saddle River, NJ: Prentice Hall.

STEP 2: Give a Complete Citation for Every Source You Use in Your Paper.

Later in this tutorial, we'll show you where to find illustrations for proper citation format for each of the major style manuals. Where you place the citation will depend on the style manual.

Style Manual	Where do the citations go?	What are they called?
MLA	Citations are alphabetically arranged on a separate page at the end of your paper.	Works Cited
APA	Citations are alphabetically arranged on a separate page at the end of your paper.	References
CMS	It depends. • If you're using "Footnotes" each citation goes, in the order used, at the bottom of the page where the source is used. • If you're using "Endnotes" each citation is listed, in the order used in the body of the paper, on a separate sheet of paper at the end of your paper.	Footnotes Or Endnotes
CBE	Citations are arranged in the order in which they were used in the paper on a separate page at the end of your paper.	References
COS	Citations are alphabetically arranged on a separate page at the end of your paper.	Works Cited for humanities papers References for scientific papers

Just remember that you want to make it clear to your audience when you're using an outside source and that you want to accurately reflect the strength of the original author's intent in your attribution.

Questions for "Giving Credit Where Credit is Due—Attributing"

1.   true or false   As long as you give a complete citation for all of your sources at the end of your paper, it is not necessary to attribute your sources in the body of the paper.

        true   Wrong! Attributing is a two-step process and requires attribution in the body of your paper as well as complete citations elsewhere, as dictated by the style manual that you're using.

        false   Right! Attributing is a two-step process and requires attribution in the body of your paper as well as complete citations elsewhere, as dictated by the style manual that you're using.

2.   true or false   Each style manual uses the same basic procedure for identifying sources in the body of your paper.

        true   Wrong! Each style manual has unique rules for identifying as well as citing sources.

        false   Right! Each style manual has unique rules for identifying as well as citing sources.

3.   true or false   The purpose for attributing is to let your reader know how much work you did in preparing your paper.

        true   Wrong! The purpose of attributing is to allow the reader to check your sources, whether it is to check for accuracy or to learn more about what a source wrote or said.

        false   Right! The purpose of attributing is to allow the reader to check your sources, whether it is to check for accuracy or to learn more about what a source wrote or said.

4.   true or false   It doesn't really matter where you place your attribution in the body of your paper, as long as it's within the same paragraph as the use of the original source.

        true   Wrong! Identify your source as close to the information to which it refers as possible, so that your reader will be clear about which ideas are yours and which ideas come from other sources.

        false   Right! Identify your source as close to the information to which it refers as possible, so that your reader will be clear about which ideas are yours and which ideas come from other sources.

5.   true or false   You should always give as much information about a source as you can in the body of your paper.

      true   Wrong! You want to be sure your reader knows which information is referenced and which is your own, but at the same time you don't want to clutter your paper with a lot of specifics about the source unless they are important for increasing the immediate credibility of the information. Your reader can find source details by reading at your citations.

      false   Right! You want to be sure your reader knows which information is referenced and which is your own, but at the same time you don't want to clutter your paper with a lot of specifics about the source unless they are important for increasing the immediate credibility of the information. Your reader can find source details by reading at your citations.

6.   true or false   One good way to let your reader know that you are referring to an outside source is to use "signal phrases."

      true   Right!

      false   Wrong! Signal phrases are common phrases that readers expect to see before a quotation or other reference to the outside source.

7.   true or false   In every style manual, citations are found on a separate page at the end of the body of the paper.

      true   Wrong! Some style manuals, CMS for example, use footnotes at the bottom of each page instead of "References" or "Works Cited" which are usually found at the end of the paper.

      false   Right! Some style manuals, CMS for example, use footnotes at the bottom of each page instead of "References" or "Works Cited" which are usually found at the end of the paper.

8.   true or false   According to the MLA style manual, citations are alphabetically arranged on a separate page at the end of a paper.

      true   Right!

      false   Wrong! According to the MLA style manual, citations are alphabetically arranged on a separate page at the end of a paper.

9.   true or false   APA uses "References" alphabetically arranged at the end of a paper while MLA uses "Works Cited."

       true   Right!

       false   Wrong

10.   true or false   In MLA style, electronic sources are identified in the body of a paper in exactly the same way as more conventional sources.

       true   Wrong! Electronic sources often don't have authors or page numbers, so it is necessary to identify a source in some other way, such as using the title of the source or some other means of letting the reader know which source to look for in the complete citations.

       false   Right! Electronic sources often don't have authors or page numbers, so it is necessary to identify a source in some other way, such as using the title of the source or some other means of letting the reader know which source to look for in the complete citations.

Quoting Sources

When Should I Quote a Source?

Rasmussen (2003, p. 4) recommends that, "Direct quotations should be reserved for cases in which you cannot express the ideas better yourself. Use quotations when the original words are especially precise, clear, powerful, or vivid."

There Are Two Cardinal Rules for Quoting Sources.

There are two cardinal rules for quoting sources that apply in all circumstances and regardless of which style manual you use. **Your quotations must be accurate and must accurately represent the intent of the author(s).**

To make sure that your quotations are accurate, be sure to copy them directly from the original source or a photographic copy of the original source, and not from a secondary source. If your sources are from electronic databases or can be scanned into a computer where an electronic version of the print can be accurately produced, you can literally "cut and paste" the quotation from the original source in to the body of your paper. Otherwise, you will simply have to carefully check that you have accurately typed the quotation into your paper.

You must read the original material carefully to make sure that your quotation accurately represents the intent of the author(s). Statements that are written sarcastically, for example, can be quoted improperly to represent a point of view entirely opposite of the author's point of view. Quotations can also be taken out of context with the result of misrepresenting the author's perspective. For example, if an author wrote, "Capital punishment must be outlawed under all circumstances where the convicted murderer is mentally retarded," it would be taking the quotation out of context to report that the author said, "Capital punishment must be outlawed under all circumstances. . . ."

Use Ellipses to Indicate What You Leave Out of a Quotation

If it makes sense to leave out part of a quotation, use ellipses, which are three or spaced periods, depending on whether the omitted material comes in the middle, beginning, or end of a quotation, to indicate the omitted material. Be careful to follow the directions of the specific style manual that you use, since each one differs slightly.

The recent Supreme Court decision is likely to have a significant impact on how state judges apply the death penalty. According to Richey (2002, p. 1), "The court, in a 7-to-2 decision, drew a parallel between the sentencing system of Arizona . . . and the sentence-enhancement system that the high court struck down two years ago in a landmark case called Apprendi v. New Jersey. The bottom line: A much anticipated revolution in criminal sentencing just became a lot more revolutionary."

Use Brackets to Indicate What You Add to a Quotation

If you need to add words to a quote, either because the original source left out a word, or because the portion of the material you quoted makes better sense with the added word, **use brackets to indicate your insertions**. For example, if you were quoting part of the material just above this paragraph, you might insert the word "Supreme" to give more specific context to the quotation:

> According to Richey, "The [Supreme] [C]ourt . . . drew a parallel between the sentencing system of Arizona . . . and the sentence-enhancement system that the high courts struck down two years ago in . . . Apprendi v. New Jersey."

You want to make it clear to your reader what material is being quoted, and what, if any, material is being omitted from or added to an original quotation.

You also want to refer to the style manual that you're using on to make sure the way you use brackets is appropriate for that style of writing.

How Do I Place the Quotations in My Paper?

Brief quotations are simply embedded in the body of your paper and enclosed with quotation marks. What constitutes a brief quotation? It depends on the style manual you're using.

- MLA and CBE guidelines define brief quotations as four or fewer typed lines.
- CMS guidelines use eight to ten or fewer typed lines as the cutoff.
- APA guidelines define brief quotations as forty words or fewer.

Integrate the brief quotation into your paper by including it in a sentence or introducing it with a sentence or two of explanation of the purpose and meaning of the quotation.

Longer quotations are set apart from the main text in blocked paragraphs. The longer quotation is indented either one inch or ten spaces, depending on the style manual, and does not include quotation marks.

All quotations, brief or long, should be grammatically correct and the tense should be consistent with the rest of the paper. If words have to be added to help a quotation makes sense in the paper, then use brackets to enclose words or letters that you add and ellipses to indicate words or sentences that have been left out of the middle or end of a quotation.

For example, for briefer quotes, quote the material, using quotation marks, within the paragraph in which it's being quoted.

> The Apprendi case is likely to have a significant impact on how state judges apply the death penalty. According to Richey, "A much anticipated revolution in criminal sentencing just became a lot more revolutionary."

18

In APA format, if the quoted material is longer than forty words, indent the quoted material without quotations marks.

> The recent Supreme Court decision is likely to have a significant impact on how state judges apply the death penalty. According to Richey:
>
> > The court, in a 7-to-2 decision, drew a parallel between the sentencing system of Arizona (and by extension eight states with similar systems), and the sentence-enhancement system that the high court struck down two years ago in a landmark case called Apprendi v. New Jersey. The bottom line: A much anticipated revolution in criminal sentencing just became a lot more revolutionary.

So, quote material properly when a quote will say things better than you can say them in your own words, but make sure your quotes are accurate and contextually consistent with the original work. Refer to the appropriate style manual for specific questions about quotations that are not answered here. Remember, too, that you don't always have to quote material. You may also want to paraphrase or summarize it.

Questions for "Quoting Sources"

1. true or false   It is always better to quote a source than to simply paraphrase or
                    summarize it.

        true   Wrong! Use quotations only when the original words are specially
                precise, clear, powerful, or vivid. Otherwise, paraphrase or summarize the
                source.

        false   Right! Use quotations only when the original words are specially
                precise, clear, powerful, or vivid. Otherwise, paraphrase or summarize the
                source.

2. true or false   There is one cardinal rule for quoting sources—your quotations must be
                    accurate.

        true   Wrong! It is possible to accurately quote a source and still take it out of
                context. The second cardinal rule is that your quotations must accurately
                represent the intent of the author(s).

        false   Right! It is possible to accurately quote a source and still take it out of
                context. The second cardinal rule is that your quotations must accurately
                represent the intent of the author(s).

3. true or false   Ellipses are used to indicate part of a quotation that has been left out in the
                    middle or at the end of the quoted material.

        true   Right!

        false   Wrong!

4. true or false   Brackets, as well as ellipses, are used to indicate part of a quotation that
                    has been left out in the middle of quoted material.

        true   Wrong! Brackets are used to indicate material that has been added to a
                quotation to make it grammatically correct, consistent with the tense of the
                rest of the paper, or in some other way clearer to the reader.

        false   Right! Brackets are used to indicate material that has been added to a
                quotation to make it grammatically correct, consistent with the tense of the
                rest of the paper, or in some other way clearer to the reader.

5.   true or false   A lengthy quotation, which must be set apart from the main text in clocked paragraphs, is any quotation over forty words in length.

        true   Wrong! It depends on the style manual being used. MLA and CBE guidelines are four more typed lines. CMS guidelines require blocking for eight to ten lines. APA guidelines use forty words as the dividing line between short and long quotations.

        false   Right! It depends on the style manual being used. MLA and CBE guidelines are four more typed lines. CMS guidelines require blocking for eight to ten lines. APA guidelines use forty words as the dividing line between short and long quotations.

Paraphrasing

What is a Paraphrase?

A paraphrase is simply a restatement of a source's words or ideas into your own words. It's really that simple! A paraphrase will typically restate a fairly brief portion, say a paragraph or so, of an original source and may be structured similarly and of a similar number of words.

You might prefer a paraphrase to a direct quotation when you can state an idea more clearly or concisely or just more consistent with your own writing style than the original source. You have to follow the same cardinal rules as you do for quoting. Your paraphrase must be accurate and it must be consistent with the intent of the source.

How Do I Paraphrase Correctly?

It's not enough to simply change a few words around, or replace words with synonyms to constitute a paraphrase. You literally have to rewrite the material using your own words. One good way to be sure that you're paraphrasing fairly is to follow these steps:

1. Read the material you want to paraphrase several times.
2. Try rewriting the material in your own words without looking at the original source.
3. Check your rewrite against the original source, making sure to verify that your rewrite is accurate and consistent with the intent of the source and that you have not simply shuffled a few words around.

Make sure that you make it clear to the reader where your paraphrase begins and ends and where your own ideas or comments are included. Don't be afraid to put the original source's unique terms or phrases in quotation marks as part of your paraphrase. In all cases, remember to identify that you are referring to an outside source in the body of your paper and to provide a complete source at the appropriate place in your paper.

It is not inappropriate to abbreviate the paraphrase from the original source if the material that is left out is not essential to the point you're making or to understanding the paraphrase. This is similar to using ellipses to leave out irrelevant or unimportant material, but you don't have to indicate what has been left out.

Some Examples of Incorrect and Correct Paraphrasing

From the Original

Although the high court declined to extend its Apprendi reasoning to strike down minimum mandatory sentencing schemes in a related case also announced Monday, the court's ruling in the death-penalty case is expected to trigger a fresh barrage of appeals in state and federal courts nationwide. (Richey 2002, p. 2)

An Incorrect Paraphrase (not enough different from the original)

Richey (2002, p. 2) reported that the Supreme Court didn't extend the reasoning of Apprendi to strike down the sentencing laws in another case reported a couple of days ago, but that the new case will probably result in a number of new appeals in state and federal courts across the country.

An Incorrect Paraphrase (not accurate)

Richey (2002, p. 2) says that the Supreme Court might as well have applied the Apprendi case to strike down "sentencing schemes" in other states, since the new case is likely to have the same effect.

An Accurate Paraphrase

Richey (2002, p. 2) predicts that the current Supreme Court ruling on a death penalty sentencing case will nonetheless be likely to encourage widespread state and federal court appeals to cases involving minimum mandatory sentencing schemes."

Summarizing

A summary is a restatement of the main ideas of a source that is written in your own words. Typically, a summary will abbreviate more information than a paraphrase, and can abbreviate as little as a few paragraphs, or as much as a chapter or even an entire book.

The most important things to remember when summarizing an outside source are:
1. Make sure your summary is accurate.
2. Make sure your summary represents the intent of the source you're using.
3. Make sure that you properly attribute the source immediately after the summarized material in the body of your paper as well as in your notes or references.

Citing Electronic Sources

Many electronic sources, such as Web sites, chat rooms, listservs, and so on, do not have the kind of information which has traditionally been required for a source citation. Many Web pages, for example, don't have authors or even dates. How do you document a conversation held in a chat room? New forms and forums for information are being created all the time that do not have established formats for proper citation.

There are two excellent sources for keeping up to date with the format changes for various non-traditional sources:

One such source is the *Columbia Guide to Online Style* (*COS*) published by the Columbia University Press. This style manual keeps up-to-date information on the proper way to cite electronic sources in humanities (*MLA* and *Chicago*) or social science (*APA* and *CBE*) formats. Their basic online style guide, which includes tips on how to document sources within the text as well as in the citations, can be found at:

http://www.columbia.edu/cu/cup/cgos/idx_basic.html

Your school or local library is likely to have a copy of the *COS Guide*. If not, for information on how to buy this manual, go to

http://www.columbia.edu/cu/cup/sales/index.html

Another excellent online source for learning how to document electronic source in *APA* format can be found at:

http://www.apastyle.org/elecref.html .

Using Proper Citation Format

Your instructor is likely to require you to use a specific style manual. If not, choose a style manual that is appropriate for the discipline in which you're writing. Your college and public libraries are likely to have copies available for each of the style manuals discussed below.

Pearson Education's *Content Select Research Database* provides an excellent guide to the MLA, APA, CMS, and CBE style guides, and can be accessed for free at:

http://contentselect.pearsoned.com/

MLA

In the humanities, high school and college undergraduate writers typically rely on the *MLA Handbook for Writers of Research Papers*, 5th edition (1999) by Joseph Gibaldi. The Modern Language Association (MLA) does not publish their manual on line, although they do provide updates at their site, which can be accessed through their website at:

http://www.mla.org/

Pearson Education's

Many colleges provide templates for MLA format. An excellent choice is from Purdue University's Online Writing Lab (OWL) which is located at:

http://owl.english.purdue.edu/handouts/research/r_mla.html

APA

The American Psychological Association (APA) style guide, used widely in the social sciences, is titled *The Publication Manual of the American Psychological Association*, 5th edition (2001). To obtain your own copy of the manual will require you to purchase one, but updates are available for free through their website, which is at:

http://www.apastyle.org/

For an online guide to APA formatting, visit Purdue's APA template which can be found at:

http://owl.english.purdue.edu/handouts/research/r_apa.html

CMS

The Chicago Manual of Style (CMS), 14th edition (1993), is preferred by writers in the humanities (except for literature) who prefer to use footnotes or endnotes rather than names and dates embedded in the document. This manual is available through the University of Chicago Press website and includes updates and answers to frequently asked questions (FAQs):

http://www.press.uchicago.edu/Misc/Chicago/cmosfaq/cmosfaq.html

The University of Wisconsin-Madison has an excellent online handbook for helping a writer use the CMS note-style format for papers:

http://www.wisc.edu/writing/Handbook/DocChicago.html

CBE and Science Field Style Manuals

Writers in the natural sciences (physics, chemistry, biology) applied sciences (technology), and mathematics, tend to use specialized style manuals designed to accommodate the particular needs of their respective disciplines. A general scientific style guide that is widely referred to is *Scientific Style and Format: The CBE Manual for Authors, Editors, and Publishers,* 6th edition (1994). The organization that prepared this guide, formerly named the Council of Biology Editors, is currently identified as The Council of Science Editors. The website from which their manual can be purchased is:

http://www.councilscienceeditors.org/pubs_ssf.shtml

The University of Wisconsin-Madison for CBE style can be accessed at:

http://www.wisc.edu/writing/Handbook/DocCBE6.html

For a detailed list of style guides in other specific scientific disciplines, refer to Claremont College's library page titled, "Guide to a scientific writing style," located at:

http://voxlibris.claremont.edu/research/lrs/science_cit.htm#style

For More Information About How to Avoid Plagiarism

One way to look at plagiarism in the academic setting is to study what academics are thinking about the subject. Plagiarism.org is a website which bills itself as, "The online resource for educators concerned with the growing problem of Internet plagiarism." The site, which includes a number of articles on plagiarism, is located at:

http://www.plagiarism.org/

Some excellent academic sites that include helpful information about plagiarism, including links to other sites, are:

University of Indiana
http://www.indiana.edu/~wts/wts/plagiarism.html

University of California at Davis
http://sja.ucdavis.edu/avoid.htm

Purdue University
http://owl.english.purdue.edu/handouts/research/r_plagiar.html

Rutgers University
http://newark.rutgers.edu/~ehrlich/plagiarism598.html

Northwestern University
http://www.northwestern.edu/uacc/plagiar.html

Georgetown University
http://www.georgetown.edu/honor/plagiarism.html